W9-DBK-112

WATER SHED

Renée Gregorio

WATER SHED
Aikido Tanka

TRES CHICAS BOOKS

Thanks to J.N. Reilly and Ira Cohen,
editors of the anthology, *Shamanic Warriors Now Poets,*
R & R Publishing, Glasgow, Scotland,
where many of these tanka first appeared in 2003.

Book design: JB Bryan and Renée Gregorio

Set in Joanna

Cover Art: "Spiraling Shape", a linoleum cut by Katura Reynolds

Author photograph (with Takashi Tokunaga) by James Black

ISBN: 1-893003-06-X

Tres Chicas Books
12C Eckards Way
Española, New Mexico 87532

no masters only you the master is you
wonderful no?
IKKYU

For how long did I stand in the house of this body
And stare at the road?
MIRABAI

The water is clear all the way down.
Nothing ever polished it. That is the way it is.
KEIZAN JOKIN

CONTENTS

PREFACE

Aikido literally means the way of harmony. An intricate series of pins, throws and circular movements, Aikido teaches one to get out of the way and neutralize an attack. By its very nature, it has the potential to change disagreement into agreement, violence into acceptance. Through the practice, I have learned a lot about the resistance stored in my body. I've learned to break down this resistance and, even in the face of fear, be open, centered, present, and alive to the intensity of the moment.

Aikido is an intimate art. Generally one works with a partner, practices a move over and over, then changes partners for the next technique. Aikido is at once relational and individual. One taps into the essential self. Nothing is hidden. As soon as I started practicing Aikido, I knew that it was an art that offered me more than the mastering of technique. Every time I execute a technique on the Aikido mats, what I am doing physically reverberates in my psyche. I have learned that the shapes the body makes of itself, the ways it holds back and explodes forth, all say something vital about what it is to be human.

I started training in Aikido in 1990, several years after I earned my master's degree in creative writing from Antioch University in London, which coincides with the time I began to write poems in earnest. For the past 15 years, the two arts have been intertwined—they've jostled for attention, lost and gained favor together and separately. For some time Aikido offered me such tangible joy and bodily clarity that the writing of poems seemed to be taking a back seat. But then a poem would begin to form itself around an experience or feeling and I'd be back to the page. I have finally arrived at a place of acceptance regarding the mat and the page—simply enough, I belong to both. Through these arts of transformation, I remember who I am and I shift further into who I might become.

I am most interested in the exploration of form and psyche, how transformation becomes possible through the repetition of certain bodily and mental activities. In this book I explore particular Aikido techniques through the form of the Japanese tanka. The tanka form has survived into the present through many literary movements. I identify most with the Shasei movement of the early 1900s, in which the tanka presents a sketch from life that penetrates into that life while also relating back to the self. The tanka form seems to allow this union of what is observed and what is felt. I found in writing these that the form also lends itself quite naturally to a linking of verse; without intending that it be so, one moves readily into the next.

In that territory where one body is approached by another and energy is exchanged, so much is possible. I have found that this is the space of most resistance and most joyfulness. In learning to let go of the resistance there is a shining, a clarity, a spark, a fullness through which I find my place on this earth.

I want to thank all my teachers and training partners on this path, especially Takashi Tokunaga, Jane Tokunaga, Bob Grahn, Craig Dunn, Wendy Palmer, Susan Spence and Robert Nadeau. For help in the making of this book and for providing valuable responses to the poems and prose herein, I thank John Brandi, Marsha Skinner, Jeff Bryan, Miriam Sagan and Joan Logghe.

Renée Gregorio
EL RITO, NEW MEXICO,
SEPTEMBER 2004

White Mats, Blank Pages: The Ways of Harmony

When I first entered an Aikido dojo, I felt immense fear—fear of falling, fear of not being able to perform, fear of not being good enough, of looking silly. Now I see how each of those fears were, indeed, manifested, and how it really didn't matter or affect my love of the art. Perhaps the fear is necessary. The fears are much the same, although less physical, with the blank page. I've learned that the intensity of the training or of the writing session dissipates the fear; in the need to be fully present and aware, there's just no room for it.

After I practiced Aikido for several months and felt in my body the Japanese concept of *hara*, or center, located physically about two inches below the navel, the perceived source for my writing changed. I felt a bodily difference. I can still recall the day this happened, sitting at my wooden desk on Lama mountain in New Mexico, behind the crumbling adobe walls of my hallway studio. Putting pen to paper, I stared out the window at the small hill in front of the house and felt something I'd never felt before: my writing was emerging from *hara*, rather than from my skull. Whereas before I would sit and wrinkle up my forehead to write, suddenly the space between my eyes was clear and the force behind the words came from my belly. How very strange: my thoughts were forming from an entirely new physical location.

Years have passed since that day and I have been writing and practicing Aikido ever since. It has taken me a while to realize that one feeds the other and that both can exist together in one life. I think this is true of much more than Aikido and writing, but the realization is clear and strong here. There was a time that my obsessiveness about Aikido bothered me. I thought I was turning my back on my first love, writing. But I think I turned to Aikido so voraciously because it provided a release in my body that writing rarely provided. I learned that to move from the body's center is a powerful force—by doing so we are most deeply ourselves, the dark and light of ourselves. Although I had felt a certain rawness by going in deeply in my writing, that sense was reserved for the blank page encountered in privacy. In Aikido, the rawness could rise unexpectedly by practicing a technique I might not be clear on or able to execute with certainty, and would always be in the presence of many others. I came to see what I've named rawness as coming from transformative experiences, when we are not quite who or what we were a moment ago, but also not yet who we might become, when we most fully occupy the threshold space. In both Aikido and writing, we become vessels for energy's movement and flow; when we are open enough to be a vessel, the energy can surge.

What's required in both arts is, first of all, simply showing up. In Aikido, we appear at the doorway of the dojo in every mood or state of mind, enter that sacred space, and train. At one dojo I visited, there's a sign on the shelf by the entryway that reads: "Leave your ego with your shoes." Indeed, this is what's required: a total giving up of self to enter fully the territory of the unknown, whether blank page or dojo mats. This is the most intense and meaningful form of play; in it we are made new. I remember how as a child I used to play impromptu kickball games in the middle of Gregory Road in Wakefield, Massachusetts. When that red rubber ball came toward me, I was all foot and kick and then I felt the dizzying sensation of running all the bases toward home. That's what real play is, a complete entering. It's true that as adults we are sometimes occupied by many voices. Voices telling us we cannot do something. Voices telling us we're not good enough, smart enough, big enough, rich enough, loved enough. It is a monumental task to quiet the voices long enough to get anything done at all! But to begin by showing up certainly helps. Most times I arrive at the dojo in an unbalanced state—from a day's work, from a disagreement, from my own internal questioning. I enter the dojo knowing this, but also knowing I can work out in a way that carries me farther into myself, that balances something that threatens to be unbalanced, that tames me. Once, after a disagreement with a friend, I noticed during the first series of techniques we were doing (on our knees, very humbling) that I was wobbly. I thought to myself: *Ahh, I am more shaken up than I knew.* My limbs felt as if they were on someone else's body. After doing the various pinning techniques with some proficiency, albeit wobbly, I felt my body come into itself, as if lining up a figure in a landscape in one of those old split-focus 35mm cameras. And I began to feel better.

In the writing arena, it is much the same. There's an initial shakiness and sometimes even unwillingness to simply cross the threshold to the room. There are conversations in my head about what next and how. There are questions about what I have to say. And then there's the simple putting of pen to paper or fingers to keyboard, the willingness to begin. Once I begin, there's no telling what will emerge. I leave my ego at the door and go down, go in, like a prairie dog burrowing in the deep hills for sustenance, leaving underground mazes behind as maps.

There are constantly new thresholds to cross. Both Aikido training and writing are consistently humbling arts. Both work with energy in mysterious ways, and energy is never the same. In Aikido, one is continually working with a partner in learning each technique. That partner changes throughout the class, and for the most part you never know who you will be working with next; you turn to someone near you, bow, and begin. The energy coming at you is constantly shifting. Even from one person. Plus your mood and energy level is different every time you walk through the door and, essentially, at every moment your body is on the mats. Putting all these unknowns together and working from the core of yourself is certainly always challenging. It is an art that requires presence and daring in equal measure. One can certainly understand why people don't stick it out on the mats; it is sometimes hard to see the rewards. A dear friend who has been a practitioner for many years recently said to me: *I have never been involved in anything that made me feel such joy in my body.* I have found an inevitable shift occurring in myself every time I have stepped onto the mats and begun to train. It is not always immediate, but it is certain to happen—I leave differently than I arrived. I often leave cleared, shining, made new.

Writing is, by nature, not a partnering venture. There are, of course, joys in solitude, but also times when the isolation wears one down. Gives one doubts. Makes one question everything even more than usual. But, more importantly, writing's challenge comes from the fact that one always arrives at a new door. Because I wrote a good poem last year doesn't make me feel I will necessarily write a good one ever again. It's strange business. Every time I sit down to write is, in essence, the first time. Of course, one amasses skills and ways of being in the art, but even these can be the enemy if one leans on them too much. The challenge, again, is to be alive to what's in us and in front of us, to be open enough to come at our material in a fresh way, to recognize emerging obsessions, to allow change. Its natural elusiveness is what makes writing so fascinating to partner with.

Robert Pinsky says that "the medium of poetry is the human body." In the making and in the reading of poems, we must find ways to make our poems live through our bodies. I am always startled at how different each reading is. Although I've been reading steadily from my own work for over 20 years, I often feel very new at this aspect of the business. The audience is never the same; the space is never the same; the night is never the same. We enter, trusting that what's made the poems work in the first place will, again, be evident. That we will be able to fully enter the words on the page, leave our egos at the door, and step into the territory of openness and wonder that made us write the poem in the first place. This is difficult. Lately I have become acutely aware of how many poets use a pat poetic voice when they read their work. It is, I suspect, what we think we're supposed to do, and there really aren't any guidelines anywhere to tell us anything different. Poets develop a voice that works with their poems, that they can be comfortable with. It is rarely their regular speaking voice, although one wonders if that wouldn't work just as well. I think the point is that the voice has to find a match with the work—and this will be different for every poet, every venue and perhaps every poem.

I recall hearing Ted Hughes read from his work in the early 80s, in a very small library room at an old manor house called Totleigh Barton, at the Arvon Foundation in Devon, England. He read as if encapsulated within each poem. The physicality of poetry became suddenly evident to me then, seeing this large man bent over his pages. And the odd thing about this was that in his bending he gained strength, gave strength to his every word. His voice trembled, his words shook, and in all that expression of original intent and emotion, I trembled along with him. In the library room at Totleigh Barton, already transformed by the week-long poetry seminar, about ten of us sat, quite enraptured, listening to Hughes. Something palpable grew and spread itself over us and through us that evening in Devon, something rarely felt or seen, something that is potentially transformative, if we are open enough. Because Hughes could so successfully return to the source of his poems, he could bring us there as well. He accomplished this, I believe, by getting out of the way, literally bending his body to make space for the power of language to surge through him and over and through us. Which brings me to the mats again, to the sense of receiving a strike with my entire body, moving around it, joining it, redirecting its force. When the self can step aside, we become a vessel and what happens seems to happen without us—the world shifts underneath our feet, and we are altered because we have both feet on the ground to begin with.

TANKA

everyone's smiling—
the blue mat crests with human waves—
turning twisting falling
the slap of too-much   too-far
each resistance giving way

the fall as crucial
as the throw, learning to move
away from pressure
into flow, away from pain
down to your knees to gain strength

the only defense:
fall to your knees and do it fast
the wrist absorbs pressure
as the sword-edge of his hand
reaches down toward your heart

what I love is the way
he comes at me like sudden
fever, the way I turn
and without question he follows
and without question he drops

Occasionally I test myself by attending a full-weekend Aikido seminar. Under the telescopic gaze of the visiting sensei, I see parts of myself I cannot see with my own naked eye. After such encounters, I am not who I was before. I think of my Thai silk robe, how many washings it needs to become itself, the ways of its softening. I think of the wood floors of my house, the days I have spent rubbing a milky liquid soap into its surface to bring up its shine. Being down on the floor made me see its blemishes, its raised nails, its gashes. I became intimate with that wood. How my body loved that work, its persistent circling and dwelling.

> gravity's presence
> pulls my limbs toward the ground
> I move in tight circles
> like water around a tree-branch
> spinning beyond what obstructs

contemplating if
there's a way to get it right
repeating *ikkyo*
endless loop of practice
I pin you   you pin me

I want to go straight in—
if I get the angle right,
wrist above elbow,
tangle of other and self,
you go down so easily

cycle of ripening
wrist swept over, elbow turned
spin and kneel on ground
hardened by the crush of foot-soles
pin *uke* heart-first to the mats

mistake after mistake
you say this is *satori*
immobilized first
by the most basic pin
all of myself put to the ground

I am learning the art of falling: ukemi. He is unsure of the technique
he's executing, having me attack with a punch to the belly, what's
called a tsuki. I love this word, a little sharp word that's over almost as
soon as I begin to utter it. Tsuki, a hamster's word, a baby skunk's
word, a word that's the beat of a butterfly wing on the fencepost.
Tsuki. I punch at his hip bone, always intending to connect. But he's
moving to the side of me now, behind me, while controlling my energy
with his hand on the crook of my elbow, another at the back of my
neck. He dips down hard at his center and I surrender to following
wherever he wants to take me. The word surrender unleashes itself in
my ears as I fall down to the mats and keep my own energy gathered,
my face protected, arc my outside leg around and up as if ready to
attack again. He allows my return, briefly, then again turns my body
down and into a backwards fall. I find if I make myself light I can
follow his energy. If I shut down and close up and sink my feet hard
into the mats, I become unrelenting stone, and I feel nothing. So, I
lighten. I allow. Tsuki, surrender, and the utterly delicious, rounded
and full falling, like an apple from its tree-branch when it knows it's
ready to be released.

> I will not hold on
> I will not hold onto this idea
> I have of boundary
> and self. As all of me falls
> my lips form new words for what is

the pin comes from hip
not hand—in fact, everything
we do here, not mind
but *hara*   *put your mind in your hips*
he said. At first I didn't know how

executing *nikyo*
the challenge of getting
the hand position right
then spiraling from center
while spiraling toward center

talking at the party
he said *nikyo* has no effect
so I said want to
go outside? and I tried to pin him—
nothing nothing but his empty self

one must commit
everything to get results, yes?
he worked for years on emptiness
cultivating nothing
that approached or that departed

Sometimes I get caught in the names of things, seduced by sound and possible sense, stretching mind and body to meet the new sound. *Tenchi nage*, for one. *Tenchi*, the sound of a baby fist. In English, the heaven-and-earth throw. The unreachable as well as the grounded. Always hard to know for sure where to place one's feet. Always the moving off the line of force. Always the redirecting of energy. This time the oncoming energy is split, half sent to heaven, the other half to earth. This appeals to me with all my desire gathered around it to be a human conduit. Desire doesn't make it so; practice does. Years gather and spread around the knowledge of a technique in my body. *Ryote tori tenchi nage*, I announce. My fellow student advances toward both wrists at once and I extend my reach and his energy downward and upward in a single sweep of intention, knowing that the bowels of the earth are as far away as the reaches of heaven, my body only wanting to move toward what it cannot ever reach.

> he comes at me
> fully and fast, grabs hard
> I could be afraid
> instead I loosen and turn
> redirect what's given

we play with attack
truly reach toward the other
something to work with
if he gives me nothing
then nothing comes back

all begins with
his hand on mine   mine on his
all moves toward the fall
what's encouraged is exchange—
in this, no enemy

I encircle her wrists
from behind and she extends
her arms. I follow
what propels her until it becomes
what moves me under the arc she's made

hand as sword
its outside edge, a blade
he grabs that blade, twists it
toward my body's centerpin
I back up, force shifting to dance

Girls don't learn how to punch, so in punching there is always a hesitancy. What I mean to do is to give my partner everything I can, but what I do falls short. So I ask one night in class about punching. "OK, tell me how to do it," I say. I'm with three men. I've been practice-teaching techniques to them, but I stop so that they can now teach me something. They all begin to chime in about punching. They talk about low punches and high punches, about coming from the hip, about the other hand being engaged. They show me how they would jab at someone, and their words come at me fast and hard as their punches do. They show me how to keep from fully extending my arm, to keep the crook of the elbow engaged. I poke at the air in front of me. They say, "Yeah, that's it," or "No, don't lock your elbow" or "Yes, it comes from the hip," all words of encouragement I need to show myself it's OK to engage in this activity at all. I tell myself that I'm not fighting, no, I'm providing an opportunity for someone else to practice what he's learned. When I punch, he can step aside, control my elbow, throw me, pin me, do whatever he pleases. Maybe the difficulty comes because punching is so much about making a statement, the ultimate irimi, all of myself committing to entering a space I've never occupied before.

> I jab at the air
> lunge forward with all I've got
> he moves to miss
> what I've so deftly delivered
> as I breathe to unclench my heart

as my wooden stick
meets the edge of his *bokken*
I breathe into contact
catching and releasing
releasing and catching

if you're angry
if you're upset you can't
stay that way, he says
time after time, slicing air
with the edge of his sword

our limbs as weapons
we begin to see how one
relates to the other
as the sword cuts clear through us
we stay calm and step 'round it

I hold my wooden sword
in its invisible scabbard
poised to take a stand
she nears; my sword sees her first
all that lives in me comes clear.

I settle slowly. I begin to move freely. First with a block, short sweep of the stick, catch it, guide it forward into tsuki, then block again, higher, as if protecting the face and the body at once, then prepare for the strike. Strike, tsuki, strike, tsuki, an angled repetition, as if I know what I'm doing. Then the turning happens, foot sweeping behind foot, and the stick's sweep around itself into hasso, stick held high, base by the right ear, top held high, reaching, reaching as if lightning rod, taking energy down, down—from heaven, from the universe, from some wider context of being. And then, after taking-in, the strike comes again. I swirl around and block to the leg, combining blocking and turning, turning and blocking, the arms' sweep of the jo in front, behind, over and over till the kata's complete. Till I'm complete.

> stiffness yields
> yields to the stick—
> from scatter to warmth
> the body gives in slowly
> I follow it as if it knew

he slapped my biceps
the shock of it turned my head
you don't need them, he railed
you must feel you have to work very hard
to get anywhere, don't you?

what I learn is through
this body, about this self that can't
always step aside
how hard I've tried to be right
how tired the trying makes me

the mirror he turns
toward my face shows me myself
shape-shifting. Ideas
of boundary collapse
as I collapse, grateful

have I lived my life
till now, I ask, in some form
of consternation?
I breathe fully and turn toward
his extending reach

I begin to see what spills over from the mats into my life. It is as if a water tap has been left running and what was once a vessel that could hold that water is no longer sufficient because the water comes and comes and the vessel overflows. Everything under the vessel becomes wet, fecund, transforms from tight to yielding. The ground my feet meets is no longer harsh. Its texture and shape have been rearranged. I move on this altered earth, changing shape. What has moved me most on the Aikido mats are these moments of transformation, these windows that open up into new land, revelatory and bright. They come after days, months, even years of showing up, of working out in what is often an unremarkable fashion. They come when I am ready, perhaps. They come when I am willing to see that the ways I've moved or been in the world no longer work. They come when executing the most basic move on the mats.

> what has happened?
> now if what he says aches in me
> my *hara* won't be still
> what surges here demands speech
> my mouth opens and the words come

on the mats, I
deepen my stance, redirect
the press of energy—
one can't create a dam
where a wild spillover is required

in the water's flow
of a mountain stream, a stone
alters what surges forth
water needs no thought to spiral
around what claims its path

how does a body
fill space? As light fills the corners
of an adobe wall, as indigo's luster
follows from being pounded
I wear its eventual softness

I'm slowed down here
as years ago playing tennis
I saw the ball's spiral
every revolution proved
I had plenty of time

He punches fully at the hip I've presented forward to him. I must move quickly to his side in one swift slide of my forward leg and protect myself by controlling his elbow. Once controlled I slide my arm down his arm and pin his hand with my own, holding it tight into my *hara*. As I turn with his hand planted so, he comes with me in a tight circle. When I'm ready, I join his hand with both of my own in a downward arc, hands meeting, his wrist bent and fingers extended down toward the mat with so much intention that his body must follow his hand's spiral downward. As he lands belly to the mat, I sweep his elbow around his head and his body, again, must follow. I end with a pin, again applying pressure at his wrist till he taps the mat, telling me that's enough.

> he charges at me
> fist furled and uncoiling
> timing's everything
> as I make my way around
> what would otherwise floor me

after all of this
I make a pie and catch myself
using effort
as I sift the white flour
into the green bowl

in *yonkyo*
I can never find the point
where knuckle meets nerve
where arm can become sword
unless I do it to myself

I pin him to the ground
as if ikkyo could end
I have changed the course
of history, yes? What was once
jostle becomes relationship

what I ride is the shape
of what's tumultuous in me
no matter where I stand
I teach myself a new stance
how to open fully there

I am focused on getting my hands right so I forget about controlling my partner's center. I forget that I can do this; I can move in and make her off-balance with my own center and, from there, do whatever I please. So as the sword-edge of her hand cuts down and across toward the side of my head, I move all of myself to meet her blow, one hand toward her centerline, the other poised in readiness, so they're working in consort, so when I reach down to grab her wrist with both my hands it is not really my hands that do the grabbing. It is all of me, entire body behind the movement, staying in the center of myself, in her center. I move in a giant circle. I fill the circle and she comes with me because I leave her no choice. Indeed, she wants to follow me because it feels so good to be in the center of attention.

> *shiho nage*: dance
> all the way down to earth
> elbow against cheek
> knee in shoulder. No discomfort
> all of it freely given

it's all in the angles
his hand grabs my wrist. I move
hips toward his center
I draw his hand behind him—
off-balance, he drops down as I sink

I never learned
to like the fall backwards, when
it's hard to recall
that direction doesn't mean
I'm not still moving forward

don't forget to face
what's central, her hand grasping
your arm is the least
of it. When she turns, you turn
go willingly toward the fall

in the fall I see
how all of me needs to be
engaged—the great wheel
of my arms meets ground. It's more
than my legs that propels me

How elaborate, the ways of my unshackling. Perhaps I will always be a girl from Wakefield who wants to do things correctly. But I keep practicing my way out of this loop, taking myself away from the necessity of effort, into the power of how my body can settle into itself, and be.

> he builds his art
> one icicle at a time
> his hands crack with cold
> as he shapes frozen water
> to the brink of its own collapse

That's why seeing *Rivers and Tides*, the documentary on the sculptor Andy Goldsworthy's work and process, struck deeply. He learns from stone, from water, from nature's pulse and transformations. He's intimate with what's most natural in the world that surrounds him.

> to learn from rocks
> the breath of waves, how nature
> constantly transforms—
> he balances stone on stone
> till one misplaced topples the whole

Rather than getting caught up in self, he steps aside, merges with his materials, which are the world's offerings—stone, water, and wind. He knows all will change, yet he fully embraces what is in front of him. He has the courage to create a sculpture that could be taken away, sometimes within minutes, by the tide. Sometimes he directs a piece into its own collapse. Sometimes his work becomes completely invisible, covered by the growth of wildflowers or fallen snow. He dares to become familiar, vulnerable, intimate, related, connected, and then to let go.

> he's obsessed
> with the curved line. A stone wall
> weaves through ancient trees
> ends at a road only to begin
> again on the other side

his hands search under
the surface river rock
for the softer red
stones. Found, he grinds them to powder
and the river flows, then, like blood

a chain of leaves
held together by toothpicks
winds downriver
just the leaves and the water's flow
make this ever-shifting pattern

In *shiho nage*, from the *yokomen uchi* strike, I stand open, ready. The strike comes to the left side of my head and I nearly let it reach me. But before it does, I am moving in a circle, my arms extended toward my partner. I catch the wrist with both my hands and all of my center and sweep myself into the vortex of energy, moving it in a large arc, making a bridge of that hand and arm with my own hands and stepping under that bridge, as if seeking shelter from rainstorm—under, under the bridge, rising out the other side, turning toward the bridge once more, my partner's wrist bent downward, elbow bent back and the throw comes as I drop the center of my energy down toward the mats and my partner falls with it, backward. Here, I feel I've finished the movement, it's complete. Sensei points this out to me. How I shift from openly accepting the other to wanting to have the movement over with. I see that I'm forcing the end. He shows me how he'd execute *shiho nage*. I watch him take the other's energy in and turn it. I watch him accept, redirect, and throw his partner. But he never stops the direction of his intent. When his partner lies prone beside him, he is smiling and his arms are full and extended. I marvel at how natural his movement is. I think of waves and the wind that swept through this landscape yesterday, rearranging the just-planted seed, the compost pile, the ash and the weeds, rearranging, eventually, even the sky, turning what was once storm and hail into today's pristine blue.

> more rain. more wind
> water pummels the tin roof
> loosens the tight sky
> I have all I need here, now
> like a hoe, I want to be of use

it is possible
to walk on your knees, to curl
your toes underneath
the weight of your entire body
then, one knee at a time, go forth

you stand still, ready
the strike could come from anywhere
it's a gift a stranger
gives and you take it willingly
open it slowly with both hands

as he grabs my wrists
I fall to my knees, guiding
all of him behind me
I catch what descends from above—
a perfect stance for praying

do anything
you want to me. just do it
with both hands. be sure
your feet are on the ground
and your heart is a full moon

wasabi rises
through nostrils as I bite
the coated pea
something unseen explodes
I wince at the cutting heat

in the heat of swirl
of thrust and shape and dive
heart of encounter
I let him enter my sphere
close in, where anything can happen

At a weekend seminar, I learn that two full days of Aikido push my physical limits, and all my muscles become very sore. On the second day of this intensive practice, sensei approaches me and asks me if there's something I'm afraid of in the technique we're practicing. I say I don't think so. So he takes the place of my training partner and the second his tall frame stands across from me, the fear he had noticed becomes very apparent to me. The move is a very basic one, but as I execute it (something I'd done for many years) I keep turning the center of my body away from him. The movement is slight, but apparently detectable. Sensei tells me what I'm doing and then stands back to watch me adjust. Because I have no idea I'm moving away as I am, changing what I didn't even recognize as real is difficult. At the end of the weekend, he says to me: "That's your work for the next year: stay in the center of the technique." Because I have experience with this man, because I trust his seeing and his intention, and because I feel the truth of what he sees in my body, I listen.

A month later I am traveling in China. The travel is very hard: long, smoke-filled bus trips down roads barely constructed. We end up in gorgeous villages with houses made of perfect-fitting wood, not a nail in sight. We end up walking through narrow corridors in these villages that place us in another time, seemingly another century altogether, certainly another life. I see and smell the fermentation that comes from indigo plants transforming into dye. I buy a pair of men's cotton pants that have been soaked in the deep blue of these vats. They are finely woven and although I have not tried them on, they fit me perfectly. But what I realize during this journey, what I keep catching myself doing, is turning away. And I correct myself immediately, hearing sensei's voice. Every ground is my testing ground. I keep readjusting my center to fully take in whatever is offered me: the villager's high-pitched song, the embroidered footsoles of the Dong women, the skittish girl who doesn't want her photograph taken, the arguments between travel partners.

> the bus rambles close
> to the precipitous edge
> along a rutted road
> with holes hungry for all our lives
> I close my eyes to stay awake

No Bicep Needed for Pesto-Making

For the past two years I have been working on relaxing. See, I can't even say it without effort. Let me back up. Two years ago I attended an Aikido seminar with Robert Nadeau Sensei. He's from the Bay Area, has a black belt in the seventh degree, and I've heard stories of students who were afraid of him. Sure, he's an ex-cop, he's tall, he's strong, and he doesn't flinch from the truth. These are the attributes that have drawn me to him, though, not made me afraid.

I met Nadeau Sensei at an Aikido retreat held in San Raphael in 1994. I had heard of him before this from a dear friend who has been his student for many years; indeed, she and I lived together in New Mexico for a mere nine months before she decided that the brand of Aikido done in Taos did not come close to matching what she had found with Nadeau. At the time, I didn't have a clue what Aikido was. I don't think I even asked her many questions about the art. I wasn't interested. But I found myself only a few years later face to face with a Mayan-trained shaman who said to me: *begin a martial art*. He spoke of the fear that I carried around with me, a fear he could clearly see and feel circling me in that room he and I sat in. He spoke of it as a huge presence in my life, and because I knew what he was talking of, I knew I had to take on what he then suggested to me. I remember going to San Francisco to visit my old roommate, to ask her about Aikido. She told me to come to her dojo and watch a class. I recall her telling me about the café down the street from the dojo that I could go to when I became bored with the class, which she said would last over an hour.

But, I never left that large room once I entered it. I watched with abandon as one hundred bodies moved on the mats in varying degrees of proficiency. Rising and falling. Being thrown and throwing. Locking up each other's wrists in ways I'd never imagined possible. I liked the pace: fast but not frenzied. I liked the feeling in the room: a certain joyousness that emanated from those rising and falling bodies. I liked the silence (broken only by the slap of hands or legs on the mats), the watchfulness, the intensity. I liked the focus and what seemed to be concern expressed between partners working out together. I liked the repetition. I liked the shifts from practicing one technique to practicing another. And when I returned to Taos, New Mexico, I began studying Aikido in earnest.

It wasn't until I'd moved from Taos to Santa Fe and practiced Aikido for several years with two different teachers, that I found out about the San Raphael retreat from my ex-roommate and decided to attend. I was particularly drawn to Nadeau's teaching because he spoke in ways I hadn't heard anyone speak about Aikido. He concentrated on the energetic aspects of the art. He had the class members doing strange things with our bodies, such as getting in horse-stance (legs apart and knees bent, much like a dancer's plié) and waving our arms around, while asking us questions about the nature of the space around us, in us. I felt skeptical, sure. He was asking us to make an encounter with our bodies and to speak loudly and clearly of that encounter. And at first, I could not find the words.

But as often happens when confronted with a blank page, staying silent enough and sensing what's all around, the words eventually take shape. I might swirl my arms and sense that the space wants to be filled. Then I would ask: how does a body fill space? Then I might feel a tightness in my chest. Or an expansiveness there. Or I might sense a lightness on the underside of my arms. Or a weight. Or a quality of wanting to reach in my fingertips. Or a desire to leap in my legs. Or a confusion in my skull.

What did all this mean? Perhaps that I was beginning to see a relationship that would later become crucial to me, the one between how I move and what that says about who I am. And to take that a step further: to begin to see how others move and what that says about them. And even further: to begin to combine these two into this intricate dance called Aikido, where two bodies in space are relating to each other, and the more they relate, the more powerful their movement becomes.

When I met Nadeau Sensei again, years later at a seminar in Albuquerque, I felt his teachings even more directly and saw how they serve to help one transform, change shape. The usual sorts of things were going on that day on the mats—he would show a technique, then all the students would pair up and practice that technique. He would stand off to the side, or walk around among us, watching and critiquing what he saw. On this one technique I felt him watching me for quite some time. All of a sudden, he walked over to me and wacked me on my biceps, saying: "You don't need them!" He added: "I saw you do it once; then I saw you do it again...when I saw it a third time,

I knew it was a pattern. You must think that you have to work very hard to get anything done in your life."

A bit puzzled, I attempted to make light of his statement and responded: "Well, of course, I mean, I do, don't I?"

Unamused, he simply shook his head and walked away.

As if this weren't enough information for one day, a while later sensei called me up to execute another technique with another student. I'd done this technique many times in my years of practice, but doing it in front of a class and for his eyes made it all feel a bit unnerving. Exciting, too. The technique is called *shiho nage* and the attacker was to come at me with a sword cut to the side of my head (called a *yokomen*). As the person being attacked, I would move deftly off the line of attack, matching my attacker's energy, take hold of the attack-hand, swing it up in front of myself, enter underneath the bridge I'd made with that hand, and execute the technique. I felt good. I felt happy. I felt I fully accepted the attacker's energy into myself, moved well with and around it, and executed *shiho nage*.

When I was done, sensei broke down my technique. He spoke of the way in which I began so open and full. I smiled. Then he went on to describe my movements and how they broke down into a finish that only showed I wanted to be done with the technique, that I wanted to throw it all away at the end. He had someone attack him and he showed utter openness throughout the entire technique, emphasizing how the energy needs to keep going, even when the technique has ended. I could feel this throughout his whole body. No wanting to be done with it, no throwing it all away. No, what his body did was become a conduit for the energy it was receiving. The beginning and the ending were one. I was enthralled. Then sensei began to ask me questions about "the finisher". How did I feel about the finisher? I mumbled something about not liking to finish things; I wasn't sure what else to say. He then did the technique, being me. He did as I did, which was to begin open and full and to end in effort. He said: I am trying to be her, but it is making me very tired.

When class resumed and we were again partnering and practicing, sensei walked by me and said better as I did the next technique. But I didn't feel better. Something familiar and dear to me had suddenly dropped away. I felt this deeply in my body, like feeling our face surely must be altered after lovemaking. And then looking in the mirror and seeing we are the same. I felt other. I felt a deep collapsing. As he walked by, I said this and he acknowledged that this can happen. I thought, but WHAT is happening to me?

I left the seminar feeling utterly altered. I felt lighter. I came away knowing I could no longer fool myself into thinking I need my biceps. I suddenly knew that effort didn't have to be a part of every move I make. I came away wanting to more fully understand my relationship to completing things. What was most powerful for me was that I knew these things deep in my flesh, not in my mind. I knew them far inside myself, where they can be nothing but true.

And what happened after this one day is that I began to see all the ways of my effort. I particularly began to notice how much effort I could put out for the simplest of tasks—I had developed within myself a habit of effort. Even after two years of practicing letting go of this particular stance, I catch myself. Just the other day I had harvested some gorgeous basil leaves from the garden. I was standing at the sink, looking out the back window onto a huge field in the near-distance and the Jemez mountains and the flat-topped Pedernal in the far-distance, the sky wide and open, and I felt myself tightening as I released the basil leaves from their stems. I felt the old effort, the seriousness growing between my eyes. So, I stopped momentarily. I breathed. I said to myself: *Ha! What are you doing? What's with all this strain?* And I let it go. And for a few seconds there, I felt the way water holds me up if I surrender to it, I felt surrendering as strength and the air as something that could sustain me.

GLOSSARY

Aikido: *ai*, harmony. *ki*, creative principle, life force. *do*, way. Aikido, then, is the way of harmonizing with the life force or creative principle.

bokken: wooden sword used for training purposes.

hara: the physical center of the body, located about two inches below the navel, but also the life center, the vital center.

hasso: a movement in the shape of a figure-eight, originating in the hips.

ikkyo: the first immobilization technique, in which the arm is first rotated by turning over uke's elbow and moving the arm in an arc, then pinning uke to the ground.

irimi: entering motion.

jo: wooden staff used for training purposes.

kata: form.

nikyo: the second immobilization technique in which the outer edge of uke's wrist is turned toward uke's center, while also applying pressure to the forearm and elbow, a very powerful lock.

ryote tori: two-handed grab.

satori: enlightenment, or the moment of intense, total realization.

shiho nage: the sixth immobilization technique, also known as the four-corner throw, which involves creating a bridge with uke's arm, going under it and reversing the motion of uke back to its source, and bringing uke's wrist back to the shoulder before throwing.

tenchi nage: projection nine, also known as the heaven-earth throw, in which uke's oncoming energy is split, and uke is led both down and back by the throw.

tsuki: punch or thrust.

uke: the attacker, or the one who takes the fall.

ukemi: taking a fall.

yokomen uchi: a circular strike to the side of the head.

yonkyo: the fourth immobilization technique, in which sudden pressure is applied to the inside forearm of uke, pinning the wrist by applying pressure to the complex of nerves there. Very effective if done correctly; very difficult to do correctly.

Originally from Massachusetts, Renée Gregorio has made New
Mexico her home since 1985. Along with the practices of writing
and Aikido, travel to Bali, Southeast Asia, the Himalayas, China,
Mexico and Cuba has allowed her immersion in presence and awe.
A recipient of a Mabel Dodge Lujan residency and a Millay Colony
for the Arts grant, she has taught writing classes in various settings,
from the New Mexico Military Institute to Colorado College, as well
as privately. She co-founded Little River Poetics in the summer of
2004 and taught in its first workshop at Northern New Mexico
Community College. She has written and edited for the state
legislature since 1991. She holds a first degree black belt in Aikido
from Aikido of Santa Fe and a master's degree in creative writing
from Antioch University, London. She and her husband, poet and
painter John Brandi, live in El Rito.

Kali is one of the fiercer aspects of the great goddess
Devi, the most complex and powerful of the goddesses. As
Shiva's consort, she represents female energy. Her four arms
signify the four directions of space identified with the
complete cycle of time. While symbolizing the power of time,
Kali is also beyond time, beyond fear...her giving hand shows
she is the giver of bliss. Because she depicts a stage beyond all
attachment, she appears fearful to us. So, she has a dual aspect—
both destroyer of all that exists and the giver of eternal peace.

This image is from drawings by women of Mithila, India.